DEALING WITH MARRIAGE BREAKERS AND DESTROYERS

Pastor Deborah Olabisi

DEALING WITH MARRIAGE BREAKERS AND DESTROYERS

Copyright © 2019 by Pastor Deborah Olabisi

All rights reserved. No part of this book may be reproduced or transmitted in any form or by any means without written permission of the author.

Scripture taken from the New King James Version®. Copyright © 1982 by Thomas Nelson, Inc. Used by permission. All rights reserved.

ISBN: 978-1-7331416-5-9

Published by:
Eleviv Publishing Group
www.elevivpublishing.com
281-857-0569

Dedication

This book is dedicated to The Almighty God, The Author, The Finisher of my Faith, The Originator and The Sustainer of marriage. To Him be all glory and majesty forever and ever, amen!

Foreword

Today, marriage is one of the most attacked institutions established by God. Healthy homes are synonymous with healthy communities. The general peace and wellbeing of any society begins from the wellbeing of the individual family units that make up that community. The devil, our adversary understands this, and he is throwing everything he can from the policies being signed by the government to the various vices that destroy homes and marriages. That marriage is not as hallowed as it used to be is alarming today because for many, the notion of co-habiting holds more attraction than the sacred institution of marriage. In the face of this constant and hostile onslaught from the kingdom of darkness, a Christian must be vigilant in keeping their marriages and their homes intact.

Pastor Deborah Olabisi in this book has aptly identified the source of the demonic onslaught upon homes and the different forms and manifestations of these attacks. She has with great simplicity, painstakingly itemized the different problems, their sources and the solution to these destructive vices that the enemy is employing to break homes today. As a prolific speaker, and a very passionate crusader for godly and healthy marriages and homes in our generation, she has been able to expose some of the wiles that the enemy is subtly using and also illuminate the stances we as Christians can employ to thwart every plan to break and destroy our marriages.

As we read from the wisdom documented in these pages, I pray that the God of all grace will expose and destroy every marriage destroyer that is present in our homes, and that by His grace and mercy, He will restore all the enemy has stolen and rebuild every home that is broken. May you be blessed as you read and learn. SHALOM.

Pastor Mubowale Oloruntobo

Table of Contents

DEALING WITH MARRIAGE BREAKERS AND DESTROYERS 1

WHAT IS A GATE? 9

HOW TO DEAL WITH GATES/THE WAY OUT 21

Introduction

As said in the first volume of this series, it is an established fact that marriage is between two adults, male and female who are ready to leave their respective families and come together to form a new family unit, a home of their own for Christ.

The standards Christian marriages are held to however, are quite different from that of the world. This is because Christians are called to a higher standard of living: A holy and righteous life to the glory of the God - Gen. 2:24. This is why, contrary to whatever the world may believe, divorce is not an option in a Christian marriage. Christian couples are supposed to stand and fight against the enemies of their marriages together, because it is only when this is done that the devil loses the battle against Christian marriages.

Also, it is worthy of note that irrespective of what is allowed or permissible in the world today, marriage according to God's injunctions and plan is between a man and a woman. Any other version or type of marriage is a hoax and a deliberate plan of the devil to frustrate the existence of marriages as God planned it to be. Marriage between people of the same sex, having multiple partners is an abomination in the sight of God. Therefore, all the principles that are being given in this book are based on this Biblical principle - Gen. 1:27.

All the aforementioned, are why this book has been written. It is to wake every Christian who is married, about to marry or hopes to marry someday to the realization that divorce is not an option no matter the challenge being faced in their marriages. This book contains tested and trusted advice which have been used time and again and proven effective to help your marriage last long and happy.

This means that, even though nearly half of all marriages in the world today end in divorce, a Christian marriage is not supposed to end in the same manner. Divorce is one of the worst things that has happened to the family institution, because it leaves in its wake, bitter and angry spouses, confused children which eventually contributes to an imbalanced and angry society. No matter what your marriage may be going through, whether it is blissful or not, or even if you are yet to get married, these free but proven advice are guaranteed to help your marriage last.

You may have tried every other means of salvaging your sinking marriage, why not give God, the institutor and originator of marriage Himself a chance? Follow the principles in His book (The Holy Bible), and then and only then can your home be secured, safe and happy. This volume specifically seeks to deal with marriage breakers and destroyers, and how to overcome them.

DEALING WITH MARRIAGE BREAKERS AND DESTROYERS

For the sake of clarity and emphasis, I want to reiterate that marriage is the union of a man and a woman.

Every marriage comes with its own peculiar challenges, which need to be dealt with accordingly. It is quite unfortunate that in the world we are today, a lot of people are not willing to put in the effort and hard work needed to make their marriage work - Prov. 14:1; Eph. 5:21 - 25.

We hear of divorce here and there, even for the flimsiest of reasons. It is obvious that human beings, Christians inclusive seem to be ignorant of the fact that this is one of the many devices of the enemy, the devil, to frustrate the peaceful and loving existence of mankind. As Christians however, we are called to be alert and vigilant so as not to fall prey into the trap of the devil – 1 Peter 5:8.

The reasons given for divorce these days are usually as a result of the carelessness of married people through which they allow marriage breakers into their homes and marriages, hence the need to expose these factors and make sure as many as are willing read the word of God, to read this book and adhere to the precepts and advices there in, can safe guard their marriages and have happy marriages to the glory of God.

DEALING WITH MARRIAGE BREAKERS AND DESTROYERS

WHAT ARE MARRIAGE BREAKERS AND HOW DO THEY COME IN?

Marriage breakers are forces (both natural and supernatural), that penetrate marriages through carelessness or ignorance of the parties involved in the marriage.

NATURAL FORCES

Just as the word connotes natural stems from the word nature. Natural things are not made or caused by people. They do not need the input of any man made effort to exist. As a matter of fact, some of them have been in existence even before mankind. We do not have control over them, but we can work consciously not to allow them have a negative impact on our marriages. Some of such natural forces that can contribute to the breaking down of your marriage include:

HUMAN NEEDS

Human needs are a huge part of life and daily living. In as much as every sane adult works for money, most times, it is not just enough to meet our needs. This is further heightened by the responsibility and needs that come with marriage. Therefore, if care is not taken, money troubles and the lack of basic human needs could cause a strain in your marriage and if not nipped in the bud, it can eventually break the marriage.

While there is no denying the fact that there are expenses to be met, it is also important not to let the pursuit of meeting your daily needs tear you and your spouse apart. One of the reasons why God instituted marriage is so that the woman can be a helpmeet to her husband – Gen. 2:18b, "..... I will make him an HELP MEET for him". When a woman that ought to be her husband's helpmeet begins to mount unnecessary pressure on him all because of her personal needs, wants and the desire for material wealth, the marriage becomes tensed and might break.

A good woman does not put unnecessary financial pressure on her husband. Instead, she thinks of ways to save cost and make the home a habitable place for her husband and children. A good wife cannot afford to be lazy, she works and contributes to the running of the home and the progress of her family - Prov. 31:10 - 31.

COMMUNICATION

Communication is simply the act or process of using words, sounds, signs or behaviors to express or exchange information, ideas, thoughts or feelings to someone else.

This is a universal phenomenon which is highly relevant in all areas of life, relationships and marriage in particular. When couples do not communicate their feelings, thoughts and expectations to one another, the marriage begins to crack. Communication gap or lack of communication gives room for assumptions, malice, unexpressed expectations and so on. When all these begin to occur, the marriage suffers and might eventually collapse.

Has your spouse offended you? Tell him or her, do not allow issues to degenerate, say it and get it over with. Do you think some of your expectations in your marriage are not being met? Talk about it. There is no need bottling things up while they go from bad to worse.

TRAGEDY/DEATH OF A LOVED ONE

Human beings grieve differently, some want to grieve and be alone, while others want to be in company of people. In the event of the death of a loved one, especially maybe a child, a lot of people distance themselves from their spouses. This is not good for any marriage. The Bible also enjoins us not to grieve like those who have no hope. A Christian couple is expected to go through difficult times such as this by grieving together, studying the word of God together and comforting one another. It has happened so many times such that when the couple drifts apart as a result of their joint or individual grief, some marriages do not survive. Things are never the same even when the grieving period is over. Do not allow this to happen in your marriage. The Bible says you are one and should remain so, no matter what either or both of you might be passing through. Your marriage was ordained by God and He has told you that in this world you will face trials and tribulations, but to be of a good cheer because Christ has overcome the world – John 16:33.

In as much as nothing can and should separate us from the love of Christ, who is the originator of love and marriage, so also, nothing should separate you from the love of your life, not even permanent disability should separate a Christian couple – Rom. 8:35, 39.

SEX

God, who created marriage, created sex. It is His plan that sex be enjoyed in the confines of marriage. Sexual attraction and urge are naturally embedded in all human beings. But as much as sex is enjoyable, it is not so for everyone for one reason or the other. Some women are so spiritual that they are not ready to allow their husbands enjoy sex with them.

Once you are married, remember that your body is no longer yours exclusively. Your husband has as much right to your body as you do (and vice versa). Since marriage is honorable with the bed undefiled, so also is marriage honorable with the satisfaction of sex. Satisfy your spouse sexually always. If you are having problems with sex, pray about it and seek help.

As simple or trivial as a lot of people make sex to be, it is responsible for a high percentage of failed marriages, Christian marriages inclusive. A good number of Christian counselors will tell you all that they have seen and heard in the course of doing the job and most times, it all boils down to the issue of sexual dissatisfaction. As a wife, one of your major duties is to satisfy your husband sexually. If for any reason you are having difficulties doing this, please seek godly counsel and help.

ARTIFICIAL FORCES

These are forces that are made by man. These are solely dependent on our choices as human beings to either make our marriages work or not. These forces are the ones who come in through the physical gates into our lives and marriages. Keeping such forces at bay requires self-control, moral uprightness and the desire to live a holy and righteous life as a Christian.

These forces can be fixed if couples make up their minds to shun such acts and look inwardly and make the marriage work. They are also character traits and attributes which must be corrected and destroyed before anyone makes the decision to go into marital union with another.

These artificial forces are mostly fruits of the flesh as described by Apostle Paul in Gal. 5: 19 – 21 and some of them are: GREED, INFIDELITY, PRIDE, VIOLENCE, ANGER, MALICIOUSNESS, UNFORGIVENESS, and LACK OF CONTENTMENT. Another artificial force that has contributed immensely to marriage break ups is GOVERNMENT LEGISLATIONS.

SUPERNATURAL FORCES

Supernatural things are things which cannot be explained by science or the laws of nature. The supernatural forces which work against the success of marriages therefore, can be termed as the marriage breakers from the devil. They are not man made, neither are they natural. They are evil manipulations of the devil to destroy marriages. It is these forces that tend to come in through the spiritual gates of your life and marriage in order to wreak havoc on your marriage. These will be discussed extensively in this book.

WHAT DOES THIS MEAN?

This means that, all these factors responsible for the breaking and destruction of marriages come in different forms and are not the same for any two marriages, but they penetrate through similar avenues known as GATES.

WHAT IS A GATE?

A gate as defined by the dictionary is an opening in a wall or fence. It could also be likened to a city or castle entrance which often has defensive structures to prevent unwanted entrance. It is also a means of entry and exit, or a door or mechanism used to control passage.

Ancient cities were often more like fortresses than cities, as we understand the term "city" today. The perimeter consisted of a massive stone wall (or walls) with gates to permit or prevent the entry of people and animals. In times of war, enemy forces often concentrated their attacks on these openings, typically the weakest part of the city wall, so the gates were usually constructed in such a way that they were flanked by, or actually part of, one or more defensive guard towers.

Therefore, we can say that a gate is:
- An opening in a wall or fence.
- A door or any mechanism for controlling passage.
- A means of entrance or exit.
- An opening in a city or house and it is usually built with defensive structures.

From the definitions above, it is safe to say that the gates that lead to your life and marriage are supposed to be well guarded to avoid the entrance of unwanted and unfavorable "guests".

DEALING WITH MARRIAGE BREAKERS AND DESTROYERS

If you are able to deal with these gates in your life, then it is easy to deal with them in your marriage. Your marriage is an extension of whom you are, so whatever is allowed into your life, automatically enters into your marriage. Therefore, as a Christian, you need to be at alert and safe guard the gates of your life and marriage in order not to give room to the destroyers.

TYPES OF GATE

Basically, there are two types of gates:
1. THE PHYSICAL GATE
2. THE SPIRITUAL GATE

It is a known fact that the spiritual controls the physical; this means that whatever manifests in the physical has first been settled in the spiritual. Therefore, in order to overcome the physical gates, you must first overcome the spiritual gates. It is after the spiritual gates have been well guarded that the physical ones can be safe and secured.

PHYSICAL (VISIBLE) GATES

Every physical being either animate or inanimate has a physical gate and, in most cases, every physical gate is manned by a power. If the power that guards a physical gate does not allow you entry, there is no way you can enter an office, residence, city or nation. The Bible says that Heaven has a gate, through which angels ascend and descend – Gen. 28:12, John 1:51.

WHAT IS A GATE?

The gate is therefore very strategic and important in order to gain entrance into a place to achieve a purpose. Battles are won and lost at the city gates. The children of Israel could not possess Jericho until the city walls crumbled - It took seven days of divinely inspired march around the city before they won the battle at the gates – Joshua 6:1, 20 - 21.

SPIRITUAL (INVISIBLE) GATES

Just as there are physical gates, there are also spiritual gates. It is quite possible to enter into a place in the physical realm and to have been prevented from entering that same place in the spiritual realm. Since it is the spiritual that controls the physical if you are not able to enter an office for instance through the spiritual gate, you may not receive your blessings in that office. In like manner, you cannot overcome the physical gates without first overcoming all the spiritual gates that have been erected against your marriage. We can only overcome evil spiritual gatemen through the word and the wisdom of God.

God instructed us to take the battle to the gate and pronounce judgment on evil gatekeepers - ***"And for a spirit of judgment to him that sitteth in judgment, and for strength to them that turn the battle to the gate" – Isaiah 28:6.***

THE MAJOR GATES (E. E. N. M. M)
1. The Gate of the Eyes
2. The Gate of the Ear
3. The Gate of the Nose
4. The Gate of the Mouth
5. The Gate of the Mind

THE GATE OF THE EYES

The eyes also known as the sense of sight, illuminate the body and show what is in your immediate environment. Therefore, your eyes can be regarded as the light and guide of your whole body. This is why before anyone can make any decision, the eyes are the first to give a view of anything or anyone involved in the decision making. When the eyes sight a thing or person, it sends the signal to the brain, which in turn interprets the signal and feeds the heart with the information as well. Ultimately, desire, greed, fornication, adultery and many other sins start from the eyes.

GREED: *Gen. 3:6, "And when the woman SAW that the tree was good for food, and that it was pleasant to the EYES, and a tree to be desired to make one wise....".*

DESIRE: *Gen. 13:10, "And Lot lifted up his EYES, and beheld the plain of Jordan, that it was well watered everywhere, before the Lord destroyed Sodom and Gomorrah...".*

WHAT IS A GATE?

PRIDE: *Gen. 16:4 "And he went in unto Hagar, and she conceived: and when she saw that she had conceived, her mistress was despised in her EYES".*

ADULTERY: *2 Sam. 11:2, And it came to pass in an evening tide, that David arose from off his bed, and walked upon the roof of the king's house: and from the roof he SAW a woman washing herself; and the woman was very beautiful to look upon".*

King David who did not tame, guard and secure the gates of his eyes succumbed to the temptation of desiring another man's wife - his eyes saw the woman! As Christians, we all know this story and the chain of events which the lack of control over the gate of the eyes of King David caused him and his household. It started with lust, graduated into adultery and eventually murder. This is what happens when a person cannot control his or her eyes. As a Christian, you are expected to exercise maximum self-control no matter the temptation. The Bible enjoins us to flee all appearances of evil. Evil comes in different forms and you will see them whether you like it or not. It is left to you to make use of the power of the Holy Spirit in you to resist them. When the eyes sees a member of the opposite sex, and desires him or her, if care is not taken and the Holy Spirit is not allowed to take proper charge of the seer's heart, this desire graduates to lust. This is why every Christian, whether married or not should not allow their eyes to make them fall into temptation.

DEALING WITH MARRIAGE BREAKERS AND DESTROYERS

When a married woman begins to see and desire a man who is not her husband, she is gradually opening the doors of her marriage to marriage destroyers through the gate of her eyes. For some, it may not be lust or physical attraction, but greed. When you begin to allow yourself to desire what another woman's husband does or buys for her, you begin to entertain lack of contentment and consequently, begin to compare your husband with another man. Your heart is gradually being pulled away from the husband of your youth. Inevitably, you are beginning to open the doors of your marriage to marriage destroyers.

Not all that glitter is gold. The grass always looks greener on the other side, but do not be deceived, face your spouse, family and marriage. Whatever you desire in your spouse but you are not getting yet, please pray about it. The man you are seeing and desiring has his own faults as well. Be careful!

The scriptures admonishes us in ***1 John 2:16: "For all that is in the world, the lust of the flesh, and THE LUST OF THE EYES, and the pride of life, is not of the father, but is of the world".***

Once you are married, have it at the back of your mind that no man is more desirable to you than your husband. When you see that car your friend's husband bought for her, do not covet it. Covetousness is a sin and also begins from the eyes. The moment you see something, your first impulse is to admire it if it is pleasing to you. But when you begin to covet it, knowing fully well that you cannot afford it or it is not yours, then you are already laying the foundation of destroying your life

WHAT IS A GATE?

or marriage. Beware of the gates of the eyes. One of the fruits of the spirit is self-control. Exercise self-control always.

You are responsible for what you see. There are some things a Christian has no business seeing, and these things cannot just jump on your face. They require your express permission and effort for your eyes to actually see them. This includes watching unedifying movies, reading unedifying books, watching pornography, etc. All these are not accidental; it is in your best interest to stay away from such altogether in order not to set yourself and your marriage up for destruction. It is in your power to decide what you watch and what you do not watch.

Instead, feed your eyes with Christian movies, literature and on things that edify and value to you both spiritually and physically. When you do this, you will discover that you are starving the sinful and Adamic nature in you which seeks to glorify the flesh, while your spirit man is well nurtured and self-control will not be such a difficult attribute to possess.

THE GATE OF THE EARS

The ear as you know is used for hearing. As the sense of hearing, it is also an entrance into your life and marriage. When you profess to be a Christian, then you do not allow your heart to be polluted by the words that enter into your mind through your ears.

In the world today, there are so many untoward words, songs and news that will not do your life and marriage any good. Desist from listening to them. Sometimes, you hear some teachings and you need to search the scriptures to ascertain their genuineness and separate the truth from the lies. Often times, the environment is polluted with satanic music which are so vulgar and should not be heard by children of God. Although it may seem harmless when you listen to them, I need to remind you to be mindful of them. The scripture says, *"As a man thinketh, so is he"*.

Your thought process begins from what you see and hear. When you begin to hear the kind of music that tells you there is nothing wrong with fornication and adultery, you will discover soon enough that you will begin to think about that line of reasoning. You might begin to tell yourself that it is not such a bad thing after all. Be mindful of what you listen to, listen the word of God as often as possible, listen to godly music and fill your mind with the undiluted word of God that you listen to. By doing all these, you are securing the gate of your ears and preventing profanity, vulgarism, and worldliness to enter.

THE GATE OF THE NOSE

The nose is the sense of smell. While what we smell may not be frequently responsible for our actions, it still has a role to play when it comes to what we allow into our lives and marriages. The Bible in **Ps.115:6 says, "They have ears, but they hear not, noses have they, but they smell not"**.

This means that your nose is also a sense organ and an integral part of your being. A believer's spiritual nose is expected to smell any untoward force from afar so as not to allow such to pass through the nose gate into your life and marriage.

A married Christian is therefore expected to be sensitive and smell the adversaries and enemies from afar and ward them off. Spiritual sensitivity which can be likened to the sense of smell is very essential to the success of a marriage.

THE MOUTH GATE

This is the gate through which the thought process is mostly expressed. The mouth voices out whatever may have been conceived in the mind. The Bible says that out of the abundance of the heart, the mouth speaks - Matt.12:34; Prov. 4:23; 10:11. The heart in this context means the mind.

It is therefore, very important to tame the mouth. The mouth breaks and mars, it saves and destroys, both lives and marriages. A good Christian wife should not be heard cursing her husband for whatever reason. This is a very bad attitude a lot of women possess. When you begin to speak negatively to and about your husband, you are opening the gate of your mouth to allow failure, sadness, and trouble into your life and marriage.

The power of confession is one that cannot be overemphasized in Christianity. Speak positive things, blessings, joy, etc. into your life, your husband's life, and the lives of your children. Use your mouth for good and not to destroy your marriage and your family with your untamed mouth. There are lots of marital problems that could be totally avoided if

DEALING WITH MARRIAGE BREAKERS AND DESTROYERS

women especially, would bridle their tongues. Some women nag so much that their husbands end up being frustrated. When you see some men, they tell you they do not want to go home, simply because their wives nag all the time and make them feel so little. Instead of using your mouth to pull down your marriage, why not use it to pray for him. Even if there are things that you are not happy with in your husband, why go on your knees to pray for him about it and help him to adjust with love. Speaking negatively and harshly about and to him will not solve the problem, rather it would escalate it. Be careful not to destroy your marriage and home through your carelessness and leaving your mouth gate unguarded – Prov.18:21; James 1:26; 3:6, 8.

THE GATE OF THE MIND

This is probably the most powerful gate. This is the gate that guards the mind.

WHAT IS THE MIND?

The mind is the part of the human being that thinks, reasons, feels and remembers. The mind can be likened to the engine room of a human being. It is the place where all thought processes occur. It is the mind that thinks about whatever the brain, through all the senses communicates to the person, and then takes a decision as to how to deal with the situation.

A good example is when a man sees an attractive woman. The image has managed to pass through the gate of the eyes.

WHAT IS A GATE?

The ears may have heard her say a thing or two about her marital status, while the nose perceives a sweet smell from her. All these feelings from the information uttered by the senses are then processed by the mind where they may all translate into attraction, and then a decision to approach the said lady is formed.

Sounds physical right? Yes, but it is also spiritual. The Bible says that to the carnal, all things are carnal, while to the spiritual, all things are spiritual. The effect that the information gathered by the senses have on the person is very spiritual. It is a battle between the flesh and the spirit and only a true Christian, born of the spirit of God that can overcome the temptations that occur in such instances. It is the mind that can either translate the complaints of one's spouse about certain character traits into unnecessary criticisms or constructive criticism.

This is why Christians are enjoined in ***Rom.12:2a, "And be not conformed to this world, but be ye transformed by the renewing of your mind ......".*** As a Christian, one of the things that sets you apart is the possession of a renewed mind. Your mind has to be constantly renewed by the Holy Spirit so that the way your mind will work at all times will be in tune with the precepts of God.

A renewed mind does not hold a grudge, a renewed mind is not proud, a renewed mind corrects and accepts correction in love, a renewed mind will never hurt another person not to talk of his or her spouse, and a renewed mind is always ready

DEALING WITH MARRIAGE BREAKERS AND DESTROYERS

to put in more effort to make sure her marriage is a success. Work on your mind every day.

Since the mind processes what the other gates mentioned above provide it with, it is important to guard the gate of the mind from negative information, and in case such information filters in, thereby leading to temptation, the mind should be tamed in such a way that it does not succumb to the temptation, but rather does that which is right.

KEEP YOUR HEART WITH ALL DILIGENCE.......

HOW TO DEAL WITH GATES/THE WAY OUT

Remember it was already established that we have both physical and spiritual gates. You can see physical gates, but you cannot see spiritual gates. Gates can be locked against you in the physical or in the spirit realm. You need spiritual power to enter into spiritual gates. God expects us to take the battles to the gates. Unless you overcome the evil gatemen standing at the gates of your success, you cannot achieve a breakthrough and unless you overcome the evil gatekeeper to your marriage, you cannot enjoy your marriage. Unless you address and paralyze the powers standing at the gate of that office you are looking for favor, you are likely going to come out of the place empty handed.

There are strongholds of darkness preventing Christians from entering into the gates of their marital bliss and unless they are destroyed, the person will remain in the wilderness. The Psalmist knew quite well that there are gates of brass and bars of iron – ***Psalm 107:16, "For he hath broken the gates of brass, and cut the bars of iron in sunder".***

DEALING WITH MARRIAGE BREAKERS AND DESTROYERS

WHAT THEN IS THE WAY OUT? HOW DO YOU DEAL WITH THESE EVIL GATEKEEPERS?

1. Establish your own private home.

Gen. 2:24, "Therefore, shall a man leave his father and his mother, and shall cleave unto his wife: and they shall be one flesh".

In the above scripture, the man and woman upon marriage are expected to leave their parents and cleave to one another thereby establishing their own home. According to this verse, the man is expected to leave his birth family and start a whole new family, a new life with his wife. As much as it is possible, a man and a woman after marriage are not expected to live with any other person. This is because of their need for privacy. They are to live together, get to know each other, to learn to love and tolerate each other more.

However, establishing a private home is not just about starting a new home unit but actually making it a private home. Make your home a peaceful abode for your husband, and if any, your children as well.

A lot of women are responsible for the problem they are facing in their marriages because they have refused to establish a private home. Your home should not be a place of fight, strife, quarrel or nagging. The home should be a place of love, joy and peace. Love your husband; make him yearn for his home anytime he is not in at home. Some women are terrors and actually chase their husbands out of the home with their attitudes, speeches and actions. When you establish your own

HOW TO DEAL WITH GATES/THE WAY OUT

private home, with Jesus at the center of it, you will enjoy the joy and peace of the Lord.

2. Continue your courtship.

1 Peter 4:8, "Above all hold unfailing your love for one another, since love covers a multitude of sins".
Prov. 31:28, "Her husband ... praiseth her".
1 Cor. 7:34, "She that is married careth ... how she may please her husband".
Romans 12:10, "Be kindly affectionate one to another ... in honor preferring one another".

After marriage, a lot of couples forget the place of courtship. Marriage is not the end of courtship, but rather the continuation of it with additional benefits of things you were not allowed to do as unmarried people.

When you take out time to continue your courtship, it strengthens the bond between you and your husband. You still need to tell your husband he is handsome, how much you love him etc. Marriage does not stop you from going out with him. All the things that you used to do together during courtship should continue and not stop just because you are now married. When you stop doing these things, you are reducing the strength of the bond you have with your husband.

As a woman, you are enjoined in the above scripture to be 'affectionate to one another'. This means you should show your spouse affection always. Do not be rigid and unexpressive. Tell your husband how much you love him and how much he means to you. Show him love at all times. This will make his heart swell with joy and even love you more.

LET YOUR COURTSHIP CONTINUE EVEN AFTER MARRIAGE

3. Remember that God joined you together in marriage.

Matthew 19:5 - 6, "For this cause shall a man leave father and mother, and shall cleave to his wife. ... Wherefore they are no more twain, but one flesh. What therefore God hath joined together, let not man put asunder".

In as much as you both are children of God and it is the will of God that you be married, it means God joined you together and you cannot survive, your marriage cannot survive without Him. He is your maker and the institutor of marriage and for a marriage to be long and happy, you need to always acknowledge and embrace the place of God in your marriage - Heb. 12:2a.

A lot of people forget that God brought the two of them together in the first place and when they get married they believe they can handle their marriages alone. God is the author of love and the institutor of marriage. He alone is the one that can make it work and enjoyable. When you allow God to take center place in your home, you will realize that things will go smoothly and you will live together in peace.

You and your husband are no longer individual parties in your marriage but you are one and the same with God at the center of your marriage. Whatever may be happening in your marriage, just leave it in the hands of God.

Anytime it seems that your husband is being difficult or wouldn't listen to your opinion, just settle it on your knees. He owns the hearts of kings in His hands. Your husband's heart is not an exception. Tell God to minister to him and you will be surprised at the outcome.

4. Guard your thoughts--don't let your senses trap you.

Proverbs 23:7, "For as he thinketh in his heart, so is he".
Exodus 20:7, "Thou shalt not covet thy neighbour's wife".
Proverbs 4:3 "Keep thy heart with all diligence; for out of it are the issues of life".
Philippians 4:8, "Whatsoever things are true,... honest, ... just, ... pure, ... lovely, ... of good report; ... think on these things".

Your thoughts are the foundation of your speech and action, so you need to guard them. As human beings, we realize that when we think about a matter long enough, we begin to desire them, talk about them, and do them. This is why it is very important to guard your thoughts at all times.

We become what we think. Therefore, never entertain thoughts that are not acceptable. Do your best to feed your heart and mind with godly things so that they can fill your thoughts as well.

When your thoughts are guarded, your mind will not stray away. When you think of things that are honest, just, pure, lovely and true, your mind will be free from sinful thoughts which could be harmful to your marriage.

When you listen to vulgar and unedifying words and songs, you begin to think of them. When you watch movies that are not in tune with Christian living, such as pornography, your heart and mind are get polluted and from there, ungodly

DEALING WITH MARRIAGE BREAKERS AND DESTROYERS

speeches and actions which will put your marriage at risk will begin to form and spring forth. ***GUARD YOUR THOUGHTS.***

5. Never retire for the night angry with each other.

Ephesians 4:26, "Let not the sun go down upon your wrath".
James 5:16, "Confess your faults one to another".
Philippians 3:13, "Forgetting those things which are behind".
Ephesians 4:32, "Be ye kind one to another, tenderhearted, forgiving one another, even as God for Christ's sake hath forgiven you".

Any couple that wants to enjoy a blissful marriage must decide to forgive each other ahead of offences. There is no way either party will not offend the other from time to time, but once this happens, they should both make a conscious effort to forgive one another and move on.

A number of women tend to hold on to grudges and the shortcomings of their husbands for longer than necessary. This allows for unnecessary space which could also lead to tension in the marriage. A marriage where the display of anger is inherent is doomed for ruin. Whenever your husband offends you, especially when he has apologized, let it go. Sometimes because he does not realize the wrong he has done, he may not even apologize, do not make this a reason to keep malice and allow your anger to fester. Let it go and forgive.

Never go to bed angry with your spouse, make sure all misunderstandings are sorted out with your spouse before night falls. This will foster unity and love in your marriage. A

DEALING WITH MARRIAGE BREAKERS AND DESTROYERS

couple that goes on for days in anger have opened the gates of their marriage to destroyers. A lot of times, the devil leverages on these little weaknesses to break down marriages. Be sensitive and do not give him an edge or a chance in your home. Settle all your differences amicably and bond together after. That way you have put the devil at bay and silenced the enemies. **FORGIVE ONE ANOTHER AHEAD OF OFFENSES.**

6. Keep Christ in the center of your home.
Psalms 127:1, "Except the Lord build the house, they labor in vain that build it".
Proverbs3:6, "In all thy ways acknowledge him, and he shall direct thy paths".
Philippians 4:7, "And the peace of God, which passeth all understanding, shall keep your hearts and minds through Christ Jesus".

When Jesus is at the center of your marriage, you enjoy peace. The world has nothing good to offer, but if you are in Christ, you are guaranteed a life of peace and joy - John 14:27.

In order to be able to guard your heart and your thoughts, you need to be in constant fellowship with Jesus. Your relationship with Jesus is the only thing that can give you peace in this world of turmoil.

There are many things that work against peace in your life and marriage. They could be the troubles of this world, your day to day needs, anxiety about your future, fear of sicknesses, diseases, death and pestilence, but in all these things, only Jesus is your source of succor. He is the only one that can give you peace. As it is commonly said, a life without Christ is full of crises. Put Jesus at the center of your life and marriage and enjoy the peace he has promised his children and those that serve him.

7. Pray together.

Matthew 26:41, "Pray, that ye enter not into temptation: the spirit indeed is willing, but the flesh is weak".
James 5:16, "Pray one for another".
James 1:5, "If any of you lack wisdom, let him ask of God, that giveth to all men liberally".

When you profess to be a Christian, prayer must be your way of life. Like a popular saying goes, "A prayerless Christian is a powerless Christian." If as a Christian, you do not pray, you are opening the gates of your life and marriage to the enemy.

A Christian woman must pray at all times for herself, her husband, her children and all her loved ones. When you pray, you render the devil and his cohorts useless over your life and marriage. A prayerful woman is an invaluable asset to her family. She lifts them up in prayers every time.

The advantages of being prayerful cannot be overemphasized. It locks doors against the enemies and opens doors of peace and blessings.

Be prayerful and do not allow the enemy to penetrate into your life and marriage. Always pray together. **REMEMBER A FAMILY THAT PRAYS TOGETHER STAYS TOGETHER.**

8. Agree that divorce is not the answer.

Matthew 19:6, "What therefore God hath joined together, let not man put asunder".

Matthew 19:9, - "Whosoever shall put away his wife, except it be for fornication, and shall marry another, committeth adultery: and whoso marrieth her which is put away doth commit adultery".

Romans 7:2, - "The woman which hath an husband is bound by the law to her husband so long as he liveth".

In the world today, divorce seems to be the order of the day. Couples now divorce each other for the slightest reasons and it seems the marriage institution would soon go into extinction. These days, marriages are hardly given a chance at survival, just because people believe it is an age where everyone can do as they like and love the freedom to live a worldly life.

However, the standard of God remains the same. It is the same as it was in the days of old and will not change - Malachi 2:16; 3:16. God says expressly in His word that He hates divorce. In the vows taken during the wedding, the words, "Till death do us part" are an integral part of the marriage vows, but it seems that at the slightest sound of trouble, couples decide to call it quits. This is not acceptable among Christians. We are to uphold the Biblical standard and do all it takes to make sure our marriages stand.

As a wife, you are to submit to your husband, but if you begin to go by the way of the world and you refuse to be submissive, problems occur and the marriage is at the risk of breaking and being destroyed. A woman who cannot be submissive to her husband is doing the marriage more harm than good. It is this type of woman that considers divorce.

All these are not expected of a Christian. Pray for your home and marriage, be submissive, make up your mind that no matter the challenge you face in your marriage, divorce is not an option. Make up your mind to make a success of your marriage, do so prayerfully and you will have a blissful marriage.

9. Keep the family circle closed tightly.

Exodus 20:14, "Thou shalt not commit adultery".

Proverbs 31:11 - 12, "The heart of her husband doth safely trust in her. ... She will do him good and not evil all the days of her life".

Malachi 2:14, "The Lord hath been witness between thee and the wife of thy youth, against whom thou hast dealt treacherously".

Proverbs 6:24-29, "Keep thee from the evil woman. ... Lust not after her beauty in thine heart; neither let her take thee with her eyelids. ... Can a man take fire in his bosom and his clothes not be burned? ... So he that goeth in to his neighbour's wife; whosoever toucheth her shall not be innocent".

When you make your marriage your priority, you will not jeopardize the joy and peace of your marriage for anything. For a marriage to work and a home to be blissful, the family circle must be tightly closed. The couple must not give room for temptation or external forces in form of infidelity. When a woman gives room to unnecessary quarrels and strife with her husband, it could lead him to finding succor in another woman.

This is why it was discussed earlier, the need not to allow quarrels between any couple. Do not go to bed angry and do not tell people who cannot give godly advice about your marital problems.

Keep your marriage like a tightly knit scarf such that no one and nothing can come between you both. When you are

DEALING WITH MARRIAGE BREAKERS AND DESTROYERS

close to each other and there is no room for interference, you will enjoy peace and none of the parties will fall into temptation. When a marriage is blissful, there is hardly any means for strangers to come in. The husband is happy and constantly in love with his wife and he has no need or use for any other woman out there.

A godly and submissive woman enjoys her husband and marriage because the husband loves her and is always proud of her. Her children are equally well groomed and the home is a stable, godly home - Proverbs 31:10 - end.

10. God describes love make it your daily goal to measure up.

1 Corinthians 13:4 - 7, "Love is forbearing and kind. Love knows no jealousy. Love does not brag is not conceited. She is not unmannerly, nor selfish, nor irritable, nor mindful of wrongs. She does not rejoice in injustice, but joyfully sides with the truth. She can overlook faults. She is full of trust, full of hope, full of endurance".

A woman and wife, who claims to love her husband as commanded has one major responsibility - to love her husband in all ways. From the above scripture, we see the different attributes of love. God, who is the creator of love, also describes what it means to actually love. Love is never jealous. Infact, jealousy is a destroyer of love! It causes unnecessary suspicion and strife. When a woman is overly jealous, she is insecure and begins to see what is not there. She keeps trailing her husband, she does not trust him. Some people claim jealousy is a sign of love. This is not true. A Christian woman should trust her husband explicitly and not doubt him, especially when she is married to a genuinely born again man. Jealousy has ruined a lot of marriages. Do not allow it to ruin yours as well.

Even when her husband and children are proud of her, she is not conceited or proud. She carries herself with dignity and humility. She accepts her husband as the head of the home and follows his lead at all times.

Also, a godly woman is well mannered, selfless and not selfish. She is not irritable or touchy, but rather she is accommodating and loving to all those that are around her.

A good number of women that lost their homes are in that position because they were mindful of wrongs. That is to say that they held on to offences, grudges and grievances. They do not forgive their husbands of any wrongdoing, but rather hold on to such and use it against them. This aids in destroying the love and bond that ought to hold their marriage together on the long run.

Finally, be a good woman, who is full of trust for her husband, be hopeful and supportive, deal with your spouse faithfully and truthfully. Endure in the face of challenges and you will enjoy your marriage.

11. Remember that criticism and nagging destroy love.

Colossians 3:19, "Husbands, love your wives, and be not bitter against them".
Proverbs 21:19, "It is better to dwell in the wilderness, than with a contentious and an angry woman".
Proverbs 27:15, "A continual dropping in a very rainy day and a contentious woman are alike".
Matthew 7:3, "Why beholdest thou the mote [splinter] that is in thy brother's eye, but considerest not the beam [whole board] that is in thine own eye?".
1 Corinthians13:4, "Love ... looks for a way of being constructive".

In marriage, the earlier both parties realize that neither of them is perfect the better. It is only after they come to this realization, that they can fully accept each other flaws and shortcomings even as they work towards perfection in Christ Jesus.

However, when a spouse feels the need to criticize, analyze and over analyze the other's behaviors, methods, and other attributes, then trouble is brewing.

While it is good to correct one another in love, care must be taken not to cross the line between correction and nagging. Constructive criticism is different from hurtful criticism. There are ways you can correct your spouse without making them feel less human or little. You cannot continue to complain about everything your spouse does and expect him to be full of love and praises for you. No, he will after some time begin to get angry and resentful once he overcomes the feeling of being constantly put down. When someone a gets to this phase or feels this way about someone they love, then, only the grace of God can restore the love they once had for each other.

In other words, every married person, instead of highlighting their partners' shortcomings should seek to see the good in them, appreciate them, and also look inwards, bearing in mind that they also are not perfect. Then they should work on themselves as well in order to become better versions of who they are.

If everyone who is married can do as said above, then we all would be better versions of ourselves, see less of each other's faults, focus more on loving and pulling each other up, complain, nag and criticize less.

What we have once this balance is reached, is bliss, not only in our marriages but also in all other relationships, hereby leading to a wholesome society.

12. Be temperate in all things

1 Corinthians 9:25, "Every man that striveth for the mastery is temperate in all things".
1 Corinthians 13:5, "Love ... does not pursue selfish advantage".
1 Corinthians 10:31, "Whether therefore ye eat, or drink, or whatsoever ye do, do all to the glory of God".
1 Corinthians 9:27, "I keep under my body, and bring it into subjection".
2 Thessalonians 3:10, "If any would not work, neither should he eat".
Hebrews 13:4, "Marriage is honourable in all, and the bed undefiled".
Romans 6:12 - 13, "Let not sin therefore reign in your mortal body, that ye should obey it in the lusts thereof. Neither yield ye your members as instruments of unrighteousness unto sin".

Being temperate means to exercise self-control, anyone without self-control is a disaster waiting to happen, a loose cannon so to speak. A Christian is supposed to exhibit self-control in all aspects of his/her life. Self-control is a fruit of the spirit and it helps a believer to avoid sin.

It is a known fact that while certain things are good, but when they are done or consumed excessively, they lose their essence. For instance, as good as food is and no one can survive long without it, too much of it is gluttony which could lead to series of health problems. So also is the craving for sex, which if not controlled will lead to adultery. A Christian

DEALING WITH MARRIAGE BREAKERS AND DESTROYERS

must be able to exercise restraint, particularly when it comes to pleasure in order not to fall into temptation and ruin his or her life and marriage.

It is the lack of self-control that makes sin have dominion over a child of God. In order to be self-controlled, you need to submit your total being under the tutelage of the Holy Spirit so that you can learn self-control.

A woman who cannot control her spending depletes her family's funds on trivial and worldly things, most especially fashion. When genuine needs therefore arise and there is no money for them to meet up, the quarrels, blame games, and fighting begins. When all these begin to surface in a marriage, your guess is as good as mine, as to where the marriage is heading.

Be temperate, you do not have to succumb to every of your craving or wants, some things can wait. You do not have to say everything that comes to your mind. Hurtful words can never be taken back. Be calm, and exercise restraint. Your life and marriage will be better for it.

13. Be clean, modest, orderly, and dutiful.

1 Timothy 2:9, "In like manner also, that women adorn themselves in modest apparel".

Proverbs 31:13, 15, 27, "She ... works with willing hands", She rises while it is yet night and provides food for her household", "She looks well to the ways of her household, and does not eat the bread of idleness".

Isaiah 52:11, "Be ye clean".

1 Corinthians 14:40, "Let all things be done decently and in order".

1 Timothy 5:8, "If any provide not ... for those of his own house, he hath denied the faith, and is worse than an infidel".

Hebrews 6:12, "Be not slothful".

A good number of women are fond of losing themselves after marriage and especially after childbirth. While as a woman, I appreciate the fact that marriage and motherhood are not easy, it is also true that though not easy, it is nowhere near impossible.

It takes a smart and mature woman to plan her time well, manage her resources and make sure she and her family is good looking at all times. It does not require breaking the bank to appear clean and modest. All it takes is proper planning, money and time management.

A virtuous woman makes it her priority to make herself presentable and neat within her means. Some ladies say Christianity is in the heart, and use that as an excuse to wear indecent clothes. This is wrong and if you are genuinely born

DEALING WITH MARRIAGE BREAKERS AND DESTROYERS

again, you would realize and be convicted that a particular line of dressing is wrong.

A hardworking woman is an asset to her husband and is a true helpmeet. This means she is her family's support system, come rain, come sunshine. In order to enjoy your marriage, engage in godly living, be clean, modest, hardworking and decent. By doing all these, you will see you are your husband's pride and your home will experience genuine peace and love.

HOW TO DEAL WITH GATES/THE WAY OUT

14. Determine to speak softly and kindly.
Proverbs 15:1, "A soft answer turneth away wrath: but grievous words stir up anger".
Ecclesia
1 Corinthians 13:11, "When I became a man, I put away childish things".
stes 9:9 "Live joyfully with the wife whom thou lovest".

One of the attributes of the Lord Jesus Christ while He was on earth was that He spoke softly and kindly except when force was required. He rarely shouted at anyone with His speech. He taught His followers with His kind and gentle voice. Therefore, as Christians, we must endeavor to be like Him. As a matter of fact, not only was Jesus described as humble, He was meek.

Anger has no advantage whatsoever, therefore, avoid anything that could stir up anger in your home and marriage. When your husband is annoyed, do not use hurtful words or harsh speech, rather talk softly and kindly at all times.

When you are able to master the art of being calm and speaking softly, you will prevent a lot of troubles and put marriage destroyers at bay.

Be gentle and kind with your words at all times, especially with your husband.

15. Be reasonable in money matters.

1 Corinthians 13:4 - 5, "It [love] is not possessive... Love has good manners and does not pursue selfish advantage".
2 Corinthians 9:7, "God loveth a cheerful giver".

Money they say, *'answereth all things'*. But the lack of it is one of the major reasons why homes are broken today.

In order not to put your home among those experiencing financial strain and problems, make sure you are sensible in money matters. Couples are expected to take all meaningful decisions which affect them together and carefully.

Cultivate the habit of saving. Avoid impulsive purchase. Be cautious of how you spend and start saving. It is never too early or too late to save. You will need it in the future.

Invest in yourselves, invest in your future, and give to the matters of the kingdom. Do not be selfish, give to the needy, but do not be wasteful.

Remember, once you are married, it is no longer about you alone. It is about the two of you and the children when they begin to come along. There are times you have to forgo a luxury, just because of the future. This is a worthy investment. Be reasonable and plan for tomorrow. Do not eat your seed along with your harvest.

16. Talk things over and counsel together freely.

1 Corinthians 13:4-5, "It [love] is neither anxious to impress nor does it cherish inflated ideas of its own importance. ... It is not touchy".
Proverbs 15:32, "He that refuseth instruction despiseth his own soul".
Proverbs 26:12, "Seest thou a man wise in his own conceit? there is more hope of a fool than of him".

A couple as it has been said over and over again is one. Since this is so, there is need to counsel each other and talk about all that has to do with each party and their children.

Your spouse should be the person you seek advice on matters or issues from especially when it concerns both of you or the whole family. You must to talk about it together.

You both need each other's input and advice to have a successful marriage. In fact, a lot of spouses have been responsible for the growth and successes their partners experience in their jobs or businesses just because they were able to talk, advice and counsel each other before serious decisions were made.

As the saying goes, *"Two good heads are better than one"*. Do not act as if you are the wisest human being on earth, your spouse may have the counsel you need for your breakthrough.

Parenting also requires being of the same opinion or at least a consensus after careful deliberation. No one parent can care effectively for the child. Talk to each other, counsel each other and take important decisions together.

Humanly speaking, it may be difficult to do most of the things enumerated above, but if we surrender our marriages to God, it becomes easy to accomplish the tasks – Zechariah 4:6, Luke 1:37.

I. Surrender your life to Jesus …..
II. Repent and forsake sin …..
III. Send out every stranger that has already gained access to your life/marriage ….
IV. Barricade your life with the fire of the Holy Ghost and set a watch over your gates such that marriage destroyers cannot gain access into your marriage again ….

HOW TO DEAL WITH GATES/THE WAY OUT

Please take time to seriously pray these prayers for your marriage.

Confession - Psalms 35:1; Psalms 127:3-5; Ephesians 5:21-31.

- Thank God for your marriage, your family and your children.
- Father, have mercy on me, forgive my spouse and I of every sin of disobedience in Jesus name.
- Father, let every bad behavior that has opened the door of my marriage to marriage breakers be consumed by your fire in Jesus name.
- Father, arise in your furry and declare war against marriage breakers in my marriage in Jesus name.
- I close the door of my marriage against every marriage breaker in the name of Jesus.
- I break and destroy every weapon of marriage breakers targeted against my marriage in Jesus name.
- I destroy by fire, the confidence of marriage breakers in my marriage in Jesus name.
- Lord, quench every visible and invisible pains in my marriage in Jesus name.
- Father, I close the door of my marriage against the marriage breakers in Jesus name.
- Every demonic agent sent from the pit of hell against my marriage, I command in the mighty

name of Jesus be consumed by the fire of the Holy Ghost.

- I release God's divine judgment upon every home breakers and marriage destroyers that are after my marriage in Jesus name.
- Father, I possess the wisdom of God to live in peace with my husband in Jesus name.
- Lord, let the door of my marriage be opened to peace, joy, financial breakthrough.......etc. in Jesus name.
- Father, I decree and declare in the mighty name of Jesus that no matter how fierce the attack of devil is, my marriage will flourish, my husband, children and I will blossom in Jesus name.
- Father, I decree in the mighty name of Jesus, my children will give me peace, joy, they will give me rest and they will take very good care of my husband and I all the days of our lives in Jesus name.

About the Author

Pastor Deborah Olabisi is a full Pastor of the Redeemed Christian Church of God. She is a teacher of the word of God and also into women, children and youth/singles ministry. She presently co- Pastor's RCCG Sanctuary of Double Perfection Lakeland Florida with her husband and they are blessed with children and grandchildren.

www.ingramcontent.com/pod-product-compliance
Lightning Source LLC
Chambersburg PA
CBHW052118070526
44584CB00017B/2550